Building a Healthy Family

Group Study

AN INTERACTIVE 6-SESSION STUDY

From Dr. Gary Chapman, author of
#1 *New York Times* bestseller *The 5 Love Languages*®

Text by Brittany Grooters

MOODY PUBLISHERS
CHICAGO

Edited by Joyce Li
Interior design: Puckett Smartt
Cover design: Kaylee Lockenour Dunn

ISBN: 978-0-8024-3780-8

Originally delivered by fleets of horse-drawn wagons, the affordable paperbacks from D. L. Moody's publishing house resourced the church and served everyday people. Now, after more than 125 years of publishing and ministry, Moody Publishers' mission remains the same—even if our delivery systems have changed a bit. For more information on other books (and resources) created from a biblical perspective, go to www.moodypublishers.com or write to:

Moody Publishers
820 N. LaSalle Boulevard
Chicago, IL 60610

1 3 5 7 9 10 8 6 4 2

Printed in the United States of America

CONTENTS

TO ACCESS YOUR STREAMING VIDEOS:

1. Go to 5lovelanguages.com/family-group-study
2. Enter access code: JNLEF3XN34D
3. Log in or create a new account
4. Explore the resources

Introduction

If you are familiar with the Bible, you know how it all begins. God created everything, He called it good, and He made human beings in His own image. They were meant to be His partners, His representatives who would care for and cultivate the earth. However, they decided to rebel, and sin and death entered the picture. God could have immediately destroyed all He had made, but instead, He took a surprising course of action. He would graciously preserve the human partners He had created and include them in His plan to someday bring everything back to its original state of perfection.

The rest of the Bible follows the unfolding of this surprising strategy. In time, God called Israel to be His people, a nation meant to show the world what it looks like when God is king. They failed often, but still God did not give up on His plan. When the time was right, He became one of us Himself—God-made-flesh in the person of Jesus Christ. Humanity could not overcome the curse of sin alone. Knowing this, Jesus died on the cross in our place, opening the way to restore our relationship with God.

The story of the Bible is fascinating, and if you haven't already, you should really read it sometime!

But what I find especially interesting is that when God was ready to put His plan into motion, He didn't start out with an individual. He didn't look for a priest or a king or anyone important to be a hero.

Instead, when God began His plan to save the world, **He started with a family.**

God called an ordinary elderly couple—Abraham and Sarah—to follow wherever He led, and He promised that all the other families of the world would be blessed through them (Genesis 12:3, which foreshadows the coming of Jesus). What did Abraham, Sarah, and their descendants have to contribute? Not much . . . In fact, the Bible makes it clear that this family wasn't always functional. (They probably could have used a group study like this one.)

Not once, but *twice*, Abraham pretended Sarah was his sister and allowed her to be taken into the court of a king to save his own skin. Sarah, who couldn't have children, thought it would be a good idea for her husband to have a son with her female slave—yet when her plan worked, she abused and mistreated the poor servant. And if all this wasn't dysfunctional enough, Abraham was also responsible for a difficult nephew, Lot, whose chapters in Genesis are, shall we say, not entirely appropriate for Sunday school. And you thought your family was a mess!

But God is in the business of taking dysfunctional families and helping them grow into healthy ones. Abraham and Sarah are remembered as a couple of great faith, people who worked through their issues and came to trust God's plan completely. It was from these ancestors that Jesus was born, bringing blessing to the entire world. Over and over again, the Bible describes the kingdom of heaven as one big family with God, the good Father, at its head.

All of this to say: Families are really, really important to God.

You may be coming into this study thinking that your family is beyond hope. Maybe you feel like the only one who wants to make a change, and you don't even know where to begin. Maybe you're just starting a family of your own, and you're terrified because you weren't raised in a stable environment.

Maybe your first marriage ended painfully. Maybe your kids are already grown and you feel defeated, all too aware of the mistakes you made in the past.

Let me tell you—never has there been, and never will there be, a family too dysfunctional for God to work with. Wherever you are on the journey, the principles in this study can help you to build the family you've always wanted, the kind of family that blesses not only one another but also the world around them.

In this study, we will join Dr. Gary Chapman, longtime marriage and family counselor and author of the #1 *New York Times* bestseller *The 5 Love Languages*®, as we discover what it looks like to build a healthy family. This study is organized into six sessions that will help us develop the tools we need to do just that:

- In SESSION 1, we will unpack **the first 2 of 5 traits of a healthy family.**
- In SESSION 2, we will pick up where we left off in Session 1, exploring the **final 3 traits of a healthy family** and discussing how to put each into practice.
- In SESSION 3, we will discover how to meaningfully express love to our kids, exploring **the 5 Love Languages® of children and teenagers.**
- In SESSION 4, we will talk about how even just one partner can **effect positive change in marriage.**
- In SESSION 5, we will learn **how to process anger in healthy ways,** especially in the context of the family.

- And in **SESSION 6**, we will tie it all together by considering **the 5 Apology Languages** and exploring Dr. Chapman's advice when it comes to dealing with our failures.

As we work our way through each session, we will draw from the wisdom of Scripture and from Dr. Chapman's years of experience. We will be honest with ourselves and with one another, approaching each topic with patience and mercy. And through it all, we will invite God to be a central part of our journey. After all, families were His idea to begin with.

Let's start building!

To access the accompanying videos, follow the instructions on page 4.

How to Use This Group Study Guide

This study is organized into six **Session Guides**, each one corresponding to a video from Dr. Chapman. Each Session Guide is broken up into the following movements:

1. **Introduction.** Groups are encouraged to read this section aloud together, either choosing one reader or taking turns.

2. **Before We Begin.** In response to the introduction, groups will engage with one simple conversation starter before watching the session video.

3. **Watch the Video.** The group will then watch the session video together. Group members are welcome to follow along using the provided outline or to take individual notes. (Each Session Guide includes additional pages at the end for note-taking or journaling responses!)

4. **Let's Talk About It.** After watching the session video, groups will use the provided discussion questions to dig deeper into the content.

5. **To Wrap It Up.** Just like the introduction, groups are encouraged to read this conclusion aloud together.

6. **End in Prayer** (optional). Groups may consider ending each meeting by praying for one another, making use of the prayer prompts if you find them helpful. You may wish to have only one person pray, or to split off into smaller groups of two or three to focus on individual prayer requests.

7. **More from Dr. Chapman.** Check out this section on your own to recap practical activities and advice from Dr. Chapman's session videos.

8. **Notes & Journaling.** Feel free to use the blank space at the end of each Session Guide to take notes and journal your thoughts! If you are going through this study on your own, this is a great place to record your answers to the discussion questions.

9. **Book Recommendations.** To dig deeper into the content, check out the list of book recommendations at the end of each Session Guide.

Can I go through *Building a Healthy Family* on my own?

Of course! This study is designed to be accessible not only for small groups and couples, but also for individual users. If you are going through the material by yourself, simply follow the order of each Session Guide. You may find it helpful to journal your thoughts and responses to each section in the provided journaling pages or in a separate place.

SESSION 1

Five Traits of a Healthy Family: Part 1

Instructions

Read through the Introduction below, either individually or aloud as a couple or group. Talk through the initial discussion questions together as you prepare to watch today's video. If you are going through this study on your own, consider journaling your responses in the pages included at the end of this Session Guide.

Introduction

I have some shocking news for you:

There is no such thing as a perfect family.

This may come as quite a surprise. Even if you agree with the words themselves, you may find it difficult to actually *believe* this. But this is a harsh reality that we must embrace before diving into this study.

Perhaps you're thinking: *Well, of course not! No one is perfect, so of course there are no perfect families! I don't need a 6-session study to tell me that*. But how many times have you looked at your neighbors or scrolled your socials and felt, even subconsciously, that there's a lot of evidence to suggest otherwise? All those couples who just seem so in love (and how are they *always* on vacation?!). There's that family from church whose kids seem to actually *like* their parents (can't imagine them ever having discipline issues). And that older couple on Facebook? They've been married for 40 years—and their adult kids still stay in touch!

Today's world is like "keeping up with the Joneses" on steroids. It feels like no matter where we look, there's always an unattainable image of happiness, health, and success that someone else has achieved—and it's affected the way we measure our families. The standard feels higher than it's ever been, and it's constantly being thrown in our faces. The pressure to not only build a healthy family, but to show everyone how *perfect* it is, can be intense.

And so, I'll say it again—and please, hear this with deep compassion and understanding:

There is no such thing as a perfect family.

As we start our journey toward building healthy families together, let's pick up the crushing burdens of comparison and unrealistic expectations. Let's take a good look at these mindsets, seeing them for the deceptive traps they are—and let them go.

We cannot create the perfect family, but we CAN build a healthier one! And that's exactly what this group study is for—helping real people build real families who are equipped to face all the imperfections of the world together.

In this first session, we will unpack **the first 2 of 5 major characteristics** of a healthy family. We will gain insight from Scripture and from the experience of bestselling author and long-time family counselor Dr. Gary Chapman. We will talk through some practical ways to begin developing these traits in your own family, and we will invite God to be a central part of it all.

Let's get into it!

Before We Begin

Before we jump into today's video, take a few minutes to discuss your objectives with your group or spouse (or consider your own thoughts). Why did you decide to begin this study? What are you hoping to gain or discover on behalf of yourself and your family?

If you are going through this study as an individual, take a few minutes to consider and journal your responses.

Watch the Video

As you watch today's video, you may use the outline below to follow along or take notes. There are also journaling pages at the end of this Session Guide for further note-taking.

PLAY SESSION 1 VIDEO
"Five Traits of a Healthy Family: Part 1"

SCRIPTURE FOR TODAY

Ephesians 5:21–6:4 (NIV)

Submit to one another out of reverence for Christ.

Wives, submit yourselves to your own husbands as you do to the Lord. For the husband is the head of the wife as Christ is the head of the church, his body, of which he is the Savior. Now as the church submits to Christ, so also wives should submit to their husbands in everything.

Husbands, love your wives, just as Christ loved the church and gave himself up for her to make her holy, cleansing her by the washing with water through the word, and to present her to himself as a radiant church, without stain or wrinkle or any other blemish, but holy and blameless. In this same way, husbands ought to love their wives as their own bodies. He who loves his wife loves himself. After all, no one ever hated their own body, but they feed and care for their body, just as Christ does the church—for we are members of his body. "For this reason a man will leave his father and mother and be united to his wife, and the two will become one flesh." This is a profound mystery—but I am talking about Christ and the church. However, each one of you also must love his wife as he loves himself, and the wife must respect her husband.

Children, obey your parents in the Lord, for this is right. "Honor your father and mother"—which is the first commandment with a promise—"so that it may go well with you and that you may enjoy long life on the earth."

Fathers, do not exasperate your children; instead, bring them up in the training and instruction of the Lord.

FIVE TRAITS OF A HEALTHY FAMILY

#1: An Attitude of Service

- Ephesians 5:22 – Wives ____________________
- Ephesians 5:25 – Husbands ____________________ and ____________________
- Ephesians 6:1–2 – Children ____________________ and ____________________
- Ephesians 6:4 – Fathers ____________________

An **attitude of** ______________________ creates a healthy family.

Two games to encourage service in your family:

1. "I really appreciate that!"
   a. "One way in which I serve you is . . ."
   b. Response: "I really appreciate that!"
2. "Do you know what I would like?
   a. "I'd like for you to . . ."
   b. Response: "I'll try to remember that."

Service Beyond the Family

1. Daily sharing time:
   a. "One act of service I did today is . . ."
2. Plan a family service project!

#2: Intimacy Between the Husband and Wife

> *"A man leaves his father and mother and is joined to his wife, and the two are united into one."*
> **–Ephesians 5:31 (NLT)**

Marriage is designed to be the **most intimate human relationship.**

Intellectual Intimacy: sharing thoughts, ______________________, desires

Emotional Intimacy: sharing ______________________

Social Intimacy: sharing ______________________

Spiritual Intimacy: sharing our ______________________ with God

Physical Intimacy: sharing our ______________________

NOTE: Today's video is "Part 1" of this teaching and covers the first two traits of a healthy family. The rest of this content will be covered in the next session.

Let's Talk About It

Take the second of half of this session to talk through the following discussion questions with your spouse or as a group. If you are going through this study on your own, consider journaling your responses.

QUESTION #1: Let's recap—what is the first characteristic of a healthy family? How would you define this trait? What behaviors would you expect to see in a family that prioritizes this trait?

QUESTION #2: How do you think an attitude of service might contribute to a healthy family environment? How might making such an attitude shift prove challenging or be met with resistance?

QUESTION #3: What is Dr. Chapman's second characteristic of a healthy family? What behaviors would you expect to see in a family that prioritizes this characteristic?

QUESTION #4: Pretend you were advising a friend as to how to build these characteristics into THEIR family. What practical ideas would you add to Dr. Chapman's advice in creating an attitude of service? How would you advise others to support intimacy in marriage?

QUESTION #5: Looking back at the video outline, which types of intimacy do you feel are easiest to observe in your relationship? Which areas might need some help?
TIP: *You may choose to spend some time writing your answers to this question privately, either in a journal or in the pages at the end of this Session Guide.*

To Wrap It Up

As we work our way through the five traits of a healthy family (with the remaining three to come in the next session), it's no accident that an attitude of service was first on the list. This characteristic informs each of the other four traits.

In today's world, it's easy to think of relationships in terms of what we gain from them—and families are no different. *Are these people giving me the kind of life I want? How am I benefitting from being a part of this family?* Even without meaning to, we can become used to thinking of ourselves as the main character in the story of the family, the one whose needs and desires are the most important. Maybe we're even afraid of adopting an attitude of service. After all, *what if they don't serve me back?*

In a healthy family, not only are we individually concerned with the well-being of our loved ones, but our loved ones are equally as concerned with ours! The focus shifts from isolated individuals making life "all about me" to becoming people who are committed to thrive *together*. This is a necessary ingredient in a healthy family—and from this place, each of the other four characteristics will be able to grow.

As we continue our exploration of what a healthy family looks like in the next session, keep a mental note of your family's current ability to practice the traits we discussed today. Maybe you've never thought of family in these terms before. Maybe you feel like the only one who cares about these areas in your relationship, and you wish your effort would be reciprocated. Don't lose heart! God is in the business of building beautiful things out of big messes, and He can do the same for you.

Pray About It

Consider concluding this session in prayer. This can look like any number of things—praying or prayer journaling individually; praying aloud as a couple; or praying for one another's requests as a group. But remember, the One who created families in the first place is the One who is best equipped to help you!

Feel free to use the following prompts, should you find them helpful:

- Pray for each family represented in your group. Ask God to continue giving insight into how to move forward and ask Him to work in each family member's heart.
- Ask God to show you how you can prioritize an attitude of service in your own heart.
- If there are any other family concerns among you, take time to discuss and pray over one another. Consider how you might support one another in practical ways as you continue in this study.

More from Dr. Chapman

In today's session, Dr. Chapman gave us some practical activities that can help an attitude of service begin to grow in our families. In the time before the next session, consider trying these out with your loved ones!

Two games to encourage service in your family:

"I really appreciate that!"

"One way in which I serve you is . . ."
Response: "I really appreciate that!"

"Do you know what I would like?

"I'd like for you to . . ."

Response: "I'll try to remember that."

Service Beyond the Family

Daily sharing time:

"One act of service I did today is . . ."

Plan a family service project!

Notes & Journaling

Feel free to use this space to take notes or journal your thoughts from today's session.

Book Recommendations

If you would like to dig deeper into how to build healthy family relationships, consider some new reading material! Each of these titles can be found at **5LoveLanguages.com.**

5 Traits of a Healthy Family
by Gary Chapman

The Marriage You've Always Wanted
by Gary Chapman

A Simple Guide to a Better Marriage
by Gary Chapman & John Hinkley

101 Conversation Starters for Families
by Gary Chapman & Ramon Presson

101 Conversation Starters for Couples
by Gary Chapman & Ramon Presson

101 More Conversation Starters for Couples
by Gary Chapman & Ramon Presson

The DIY Guide to Building a Family That Lasts: 12 Tools for Improving Your Home Life
by Gary Chapman & Shannon Warden

Screen Kids: 5 Relational Skills Every Child Needs in a Tech-Driven World
by Gary Chapman & Arlene Pellicane

Grandparenting Screen Kids: How to Help, What to Say, and Where to Begin
by Gary Chapman & Arlene Pellicane

Building Love Together in Blended Families

by Gary Chapman & Ron L. Deal

Sharing Love Abundantly in Special Needs Families

by Gary Chapman & Jolene Philo

Anger:

Taming a Powerful Emotion

by Gary Chapman

The Gift of Sex:

A Guide to Sexual Fulfillment

by Joyce J. Penner & Clifford L. Penner

SESSION 2

Five Traits of a Healthy Family: Part 2

INSTRUCTIONS

Read through the Introduction below, either individually or aloud as a couple or group. Talk through the initial discussion questions together as you prepare to watch today's video. If you are going through this study on your own, consider journaling your responses in the pages included at the end of this Session Guide.

Introduction

You know, if you think about it . . . families were kind of the original group project.

As with any group project, families are made up of different personalities assigned to one another. As with any group project, there are many different roles to play in the common goal of survival. And just like any group project, there's high potential for a whole lot of drama.

Maybe your family is fairly united when it comes to building healthy habits, but this is not always the case. Many of us begin this process feeling like the group member who is doing all the work. But the group project of building a family doesn't have to be a logistical nightmare. We were meant to do this as a team—and it is absolutely possible to start seeing positive change in that direction, even in your family.

In our first session, we unpacked the first two of five characteristics of a healthy family: **an attitude of service** and **intimacy between the husband and wife.** It's easy to see how these characteristics form a solid foundation for the rest of family. When we approach our relationships with a reciprocated attitude of service, this creates a family culture that supports and appreciates one another. When there is real intimacy—intellectual, emotional, social, spiritual, and physical—between a husband and wife, it creates a safe and nurturing environment for everyone in the household.

Today, we will build on this foundation by exploring the remaining three characteristics of a healthy family. These traits will focus further on the dynamics of marriage and parenting, drawing from Scripture and from Dr. Chapman's years of counseling experience. In other words, we will discover how that group project of building a family might look when it's done well.

Before We Begin

Before we jump into today's video, take a few minutes to check in with your group or spouse (or consider your own thoughts). Recalling Session 1, what were the first two traits of a healthy family? How have you considered implementing some of Dr. Chapman's advice so far? How do you imagine this could benefit your family? What challenges do you foresee at this point in the study?

If you are going through this study as an individual, take a few minutes to consider and journal your responses.

Watch the Video

As you watch today's video, you may use the outline below to follow along or take notes. There are also journaling pages at the end of this Session Guide for further note-taking.

PLAY SESSION 2 VIDEO

"Five Traits of a Healthy Family: Part 2"

SCRIPTURE FOR TODAY

Ephesians 5:21–6:4 (NIV)

Submit to one another out of reverence for Christ.

Wives, submit yourselves to your own husbands as you do to the Lord. For the husband is the head of the wife as Christ is the head of the church, his body, of which he is the Savior. Now as the church submits to Christ, so also wives should submit to their husbands in everything.

Husbands, love your wives, just as Christ loved the church and gave himself up for her to make her holy, cleansing her by the washing with water through the word, and to present her to himself as a radiant church, without stain or wrinkle or any other blemish, but holy and blameless. In this same way, husbands ought to love their wives as their own bodies. He who loves his wife loves himself. After all, no one ever hated their own body, but they feed and care for their body, just as Christ does the church—for we are members of his body. "For this reason a man will leave his father and mother and be united to his wife, and the two will become one flesh." This is a profound mystery—but I am talking about Christ and the church. However, each one of you also must love his wife as he loves himself, and the wife must respect her husband.

Children, obey your parents in the Lord, for this is right. "Honor your father and mother"—which is the first commandment with a promise—"so that it may go well with you and that you may enjoy long life on the earth."

Fathers, do not exasperate your children; instead, bring them up in the training and instruction of the Lord.

FIVE TRAITS OF A HEALTHY FAMILY

(continued from Session 1)

#1: An Attitude of Service

#2: Intimacy Between the Husband and Wife

#3: Parents Who Teach and Train Their Children

> Fathers, do not provoke your children to anger by the way you treat them. Rather, bring them up with the training and instruction that comes from the Lord.
> **–Ephesians 6:4 (NLT)**

Nurture means training by ______________________.

Admonition means teaching by ______________________.

These must always go together! This is best done in the context of _______________.

#4: Husbands Who Are Loving Leaders

- **Ephesians 5:23** — H ______________
- **Ephesians 5:23** — S ________________
- **Ephesians 5:25–28** — L _____________; G ______________
- **Ephesians 5:29** — F__________ and C __________ for Wife
- **Ephesians 5:31** — L ________________ Parents
- **Ephesians 6:4** — L __________ and L __________ Children

Characteristics of a **loving husband:**

1. A loving husband views his wife as a ________________.
2. A loving husband will __________________ with his wife.
3. A loving husband will put his wife at the ___________ of his __________________ list.
4. A loving husband will love his wife __________________.
5. A loving husband is committed to ___________________ and ___________________ his wife's needs.
6. A loving husband will seek to model his __________________ and __________________ values.

#5: Children Who Obey and Honor Their Parents

Obedience is a **healthy word**!

1. Obedience implies respect for _______________________.
2. Obedience builds _______________________.
3. Obedience builds _______________________.

How to **teach** obedience:

1. By our ________________.
2. By letting them ______________________ consequences.
3. By ______________________ obedience.

Obedience leads to **honor**.

Honor is _______________ more than _______________!

Let's Talk About It

QUESTION #1: Let's recap—what are the five traits of a healthy family, according to Dr. Chapman's teaching in the first two sessions?

QUESTION #2: What does it mean to teach our children through both words and actions? How have you seen this done well, either in your own life or by observation? How have you seen this done poorly?

QUESTION #3: As a group, summarize Dr. Chapman's description of loving leadership, based on the Ephesians 5–6 passage. How do you work out this dynamic in your own family? How is this style of leadership modeled after Christ and the church?

QUESTION #4: If your family includes children (either young or grown up), what challenges have you encountered in teaching obedience? How did Dr. Chapman advise that obedience should be taught?

QUESTION #5: Which of these five traits do you observe as most present in your own family? Which are you most eager to work on, and why?

To Wrap It Up

As we recalled in today's discussion time, Dr. Chapman's five characteristics of a healthy family are:

1. An attitude of service
2. Intimacy between the husband and wife
3. Parents who teach and train their children
4. Husbands who are loving leaders
5. Children who obey and honor their parents

As we conclude today's session, consider trying Dr. Chapman's challenge from the end of today's video. Give everyone in your family a piece of paper containing the list of these five traits of a healthy family. Each person should go through the list and give your family a score between 1 and 5 next to each characteristic. A score of 1 would mean, "We're not doing well in this area," while a score of 5 means, "We're great at this!"

Once each person has completed this step, go through the scores and discuss them as a family. Remember to be patient with one another—there's no need to take the answers too personally! Every family has areas that need improvement, and that growth cannot happen unless you acknowledge the need for it. Keep an open mind and talk with one another about how you might change things up! If you're willing to listen, you will likely find that your family already has some great ideas.

If you'd like more advice on these topics, check out the book recommendations at the end of this Session Guide.

Pray About It

Consider concluding this session in prayer. This can look like any number of things—praying or prayer journaling individually; praying aloud as a couple; or praying for one another's requests as a group. But remember, the One who created families in the first place is the One who is best equipped to help you!

Feel free to use the following prompts, should you find them helpful:

- After going through these first two sessions, which of the five traits of a healthy family feels the most challenging to begin improving upon? Pray about specific circumstances with one another and ask God for wisdom and His help!

- Ask the Holy Spirit to work in the hearts of each family represented in the group, that there would be cooperation and reciprocity needed for change to happen.
- Thank God for the family you have, and ask for wisdom and patience as you continue your journey through this study.
- If there are any other family concerns among you, take time to discuss and pray over one other. Consider how you might support one another in practical ways as you continue in this study.

More from Dr. Chapman

If you plan to try Dr. Chapman's challenge from today's video, you may print out or copy down the list below to pass out among your family members. Grade yourselves on each category, with 1 as the lowest score and 5 as the highest.

Five Traits of a Healthy Family	Scoring Scale (1 – 5)				
An attitude of service	1	2	3	4	5
Intimacy between the husband and wife	1	2	3	4	5
Parents who teach and train their children	1	2	3	4	5
Husbands who are loving leaders	1	2	3	4	5
Children who obey and honor their parents	1	2	3	4	5

Notes & Journaling

Feel free to use this space to take notes or journal your thoughts from today's session.

Book Recommendations

If you would like to dig deeper into how to build healthy family relationships, consider some new reading material! Each of these titles can be found at **5LoveLanguages.com**.

5 Traits of a Healthy Family
by Gary Chapman

The Marriage You've Always Wanted
by Gary Chapman

A Simple Guide to a Better Marriage
by Gary Chapman & John Hinkley

101 Conversation Starters for Families
by Gary Chapman & Ramon Presson

101 Conversation Starters for Couples
by Gary Chapman & Ramon Presson

101 More Conversation Starters for Couples
by Gary Chapman & Ramon Presson

The DIY Guide to Building a Family That Lasts: 12 Tools for Improving Your Home Life
by Gary Chapman & Shannon Warden

Screen Kids: 5 Relational Skills Every Child Needs in a Tech-Driven World
by Gary Chapman & Arlene Pellicane

Grandparenting Screen Kids: How to Help, What to Say, and Where to Begin
by Gary Chapman & Arlene Pellicane

Building Love Together in Blended Families
by Gary Chapman & Ron L. Deal

Sharing Love Abundantly in Special Needs Families
by Gary Chapman & Jolene Philo

Anger:
Taming a Powerful Emotion
by Gary Chapman

The Gift of Sex:
A Guide to Sexual Fulfillment
by Joyce J. Penner & Clifford L. Penner

SESSION 3

The 5 Love Languages® of Children & Teenagers

INSTRUCTIONS

Read through the Introduction below, either individually or aloud as a couple or group. Talk through the initial discussion questions together as you prepare to watch today's video. If you are going through this study on your own, consider journaling your responses in the pages included at the end of this Session Guide.

Introduction

If you are familiar with Dr. Gary Chapman, you will almost certainly have heard of his book *The 5 Love Languages*®. With more than 20 million copies sold, this #1 *New York Times* bestseller has helped couples all over the world strengthen and build healthy marriages. (As we work our way through the journey of building a healthy family, this may be just what you need to grow closer as a couple. The book is available at **5LoveLanguages.com**—and likely at your local library!)

The premise of the book is that each of us prefers to give and receive love in unique ways. What might be a deeply sincere expression of love for one person may not be considered so meaningful for another, and this can lead to miscommunication and misunderstanding. With decades of marriage and family counseling experience, Dr. Chapman organized expressions of human love into five categories—which have become known as the 5 Love Languages®. When you understand how your spouse prefers to give and receive love—his or her primary Love Language—it can go a long way toward fostering good communication and healthy intimacy.

Wait a minute, you may be thinking. *I thought this session was supposed to be about communicating with our children? What do the 5 Love Languages® have to do with that?*

Well, as it turns out, the 5 Love Languages® are also a great tool when it comes to parents expressing sincere love to their children!

In today's session, we will unpack each of the 5 Love Languages®, focusing specifically on how they relate to communication with our kids. We will talk about what it looks like to put this knowledge into practice, regardless of our children's age. Finally, we'll consider how these ideas can (and should!) affect our methods of discipline.

Before We Begin

Before we jump into today's video, take a few minutes to check in with your group or spouse (or consider your own thoughts). Maybe you have young kids still at home or adult children out of the house. Maybe you have nieces and nephews, grandkids, or hope to have children of your own someday. Maybe you simply want a better understanding of your own childhood experiences. Together, discuss where you find yourself on this journey. What do you hope to take away from this session?

If you are going through this study as an individual, take a few minutes to consider and journal your responses.

Watch the Video

As you watch today's video, you may use the outline below to follow along or take notes. There are also journaling pages at the end of this Session Guide for further note-taking.

PLAY SESSION 3 VIDEO
"The 5 Love Languages® of Children & Teenagers"

#1: Physical Touch
Mark 10:13–16

This language certainly includes hugging and snuggling our children—but also wrestling, playing sports, giving high fives, goofing off, and all sorts of healthy touches! For some children, acknowledging their presence with a healthy touch makes them feel most loved.

#2: Words of Affirmation

> *The tongue can bring death or life; those who love to talk will reap the consequences.*
> **–Proverbs 18:21 (NLT)**

- Words of ______________________________
- Words of ______________________________
- Words of ______________________________

#3: Quality Time
Mark 3:14

- This language means giving your child your ________________________ attention.

#4: Receiving Gifts

Romans 8:32

It's the thought that counts! But not the thought that's left in your head—it's the gift that came out of the thought in your head that counts!

#5: Acts of Service

> *Dear children, let's not merely say that we love each other; let us show the truth by our actions.*
> **–1 John 3:18 (NLT)**

How Love Languages Affect Discipline

1. ____________________ Discipline
2. ____________________ Discipline
3. More ____________________ Discipline

The Ingredients of Love

a.

b.

c.

Let's Talk About It

QUESTION #1: Let's recap—what are the 5 Love Languages®? What might it look like to express love to a child in each of these languages?

QUESTION #2: Think of your own kids, your young relatives, the children of friends around you, or simply your own childhood. What resonated most with you from today's video? What did you find most surprising or challenging? What questions do you still have about these ideas, if any?

QUESTION #3: When it comes to discipline, Dr. Chapman's advice is to wrap it in expressions of love, using the child's primary Love Language. How do you imagine this playing out, either with your own children or in a hypothetical situation? What challenges do you foresee?

QUESTION #4: If you have kids in your life at this moment, what might their primary Love Languages be? If you're not sure, how would go about trying to find out?
TIP: *See the* ***More from Dr. Chapman*** *section near the end of this Session Guide for insight on this topic!*

QUESTION #5: Your version of a healthy family may or may not include kids, but understanding our own childhoods can go a long way toward building healthier relationships down the road. As a group, discuss your own primary Love Languages. What made (or would have made) you feel most loved as a child? How about as a teenager? How might understanding your own childhood needs—whether or not they were met—help you better understand what a healthy family looks like today?
TIP: *If you don't know your primary Love Language, spend a few*

minutes to take the free quiz at **5LoveLanguages.com** *so you can discuss your results!*

To Wrap It Up

As Dr. Chapman said at the beginning of today's video, the question is not if you love the children in your life. Of course you do! The question is, do your children feel loved?

Understanding how your child most naturally gives and receives love can be life-changing as you navigate how to be a healthy parent or parental figure. When you speak your child's Love Language consistently, you create an environment that allows them to connect deeply with you and others in the family. Remember those five traits of a healthy family from Sessions 1 and 2? When children feel deeply loved by their parents, it is so much easier for those traits to grow!

And remember—you can talk about these ideas *with* your children. The idea of Love Languages isn't too complicated for them to understand, especially as they grow older. The more you emphasize this in your family, the more each member will begin to put it into practice. Imagine what deep and healthy relationships your child will develop when they understand the concept of the Love Languages from a young age!

For more information about how to determine your child's Love Language, check out the **More from Dr. Chapman** section near the end of this Session Guide.

Pray About It

Consider concluding this session in prayer. This can look like any number of things—praying or prayer journaling individually; praying aloud as a couple; or praying for one another's requests as a group. But remember, the One who created families in the first place is the One who is best equipped to help you!

Feel free to use the following prompts, should you find them helpful:

- Spend time praying for each family represented in your group (or praying over your own family). Ask God for wisdom and insight to implement everything we learned today as you continue to build your family.
- The topic of kids and childhood can trigger painful emotions for a variety of reasons. Be sensitive to your group's individual needs today. Pray over any specific circumstances or challenges each person is dealing with.
- Spend time praying over your own childhoods, asking God to not only heal anything that was hurtful, but to help each of you move forward into healthy relationships.
- If there are any other family concerns among you, take time to discuss and pray over one other. Consider how you might support one another in practical ways as you continue in this study.

More from Dr. Chapman

How do I discover my child's primary Love Language?

Wondering how to know which Love Language is most meaningful for your child? Here are some helpful tips when discerning how he or she prefers to give and receive love:

1. **Observe how they express love to you and others.** Are they constantly hugging or hanging on to you? Do they often try to join in on whatever activity is happening? Do they like to bring you small gifts, like flowers from the yard or artwork they have created? These are usually helpful indicators of the ways that they prefer to give and receive love.

2. **What do they request most often?** Maybe your child constantly asks to wrestle with you. Maybe they always want to show you something, insisting on your full attention. Paying attention to the things your children request can be helpful in discerning their primary Love Language.

3. **What do they complain about?** Dr. Chapman once counseled a mother who reported her six-year-old son's increase in complaining after his baby brother was born. His complaints usually went something like: "We don't ever go to the park anymore," or "We don't play catch outside anymore." What does this tell you? He was missing his Quality Time with his mother! Of course, these were understandable, temporary changes due to the newborn baby, but paying attention to her son's complaints helped this mother to better understand how to fill his Love Tank.

4. **Give choices between two options.** Let your child choose between two activities, each specifically tied to a Love Language. You might say something like, "Would you like to go to the store with me and buy those new shoes you've been wanting? Or would you like to go for a walk in the woods with me?" This first connects to Receiving Gifts, and the second to Quality Time. Try this out a few times and see which option your child tends to choose.

5. **Experiment!** If you're still struggling to discern your child's primary Love Language, you can always experiment. Try to give heavy doses of Words of Affirmation one week, observing your child's reaction. Then, the following week, switch it up! Continue to note your child's responses and use these to discern which Love Language they seem to appreciate most.

Still not sure? There are a number of free Love Language quizzes for various ages available at **5LoveLanguages.com**. You will also find games that you can try out with your younger children!

What about my teenagers? Do their primary Love Languages change?

For the most part, a person's primary Love Language tends to remain the same from childhood into the teen years. What can be confusing for parents, however, is a teenager's sudden disdain for the *ways* you speak his or her Love Language.

Perhaps your son's primary Love Language is Physical Touch, and all throughout his young years, he needed constant hugs! It can be jarring when he turns 13 or 14 and suddenly he doesn't want you to hug him in front of his friends. His primary Love Language probably hasn't changed—he still feels most loved through appropriate physical contact. But now that he is getting older, you will need to discern new ways to speak that Love Language. You might make a point of giving him space around his friends, while still hugging him when he gets home from school. Maybe you get in the habit of acknowledging his presence with a shoulder squeeze when he enters the room. In today's video, Dr. Chapman read one testimonial from a preteen who knew he was loved because his dad would purposely bump into him when he walked by! Teenagers are growing up, but they're not grown up yet. Sometimes, a little goofing off can be just the thing to fill their Love Tanks.

Remember, teenagers don't want to be treated like little kids, but they still need to feel loved by their parents. The key is to let your methods of expressing love mature at same rate as your growing child.

Still not sure about your teenager's primary Love Language? Visit **5LoveLanguages.com** for a free Love Language quiz designed especially for this age group.

Notes & Journaling

Feel free to use this space to take notes or journal your thoughts from today's session.

Book Recommendations

If you would like to dig deeper into how to build healthy family relationships, consider some new reading material! Each of these titles can be found at **5LoveLanguages.com**.

The 5 Love Languages®
by Gary Chapman

The 5 Love Languages® for Men
by Gary Chapman

The 5 Love Languages® of Children
by Gary Chapman & Ross Campbell

The 5 Love Languages® of Teenagers
by Gary Chapman

A Teen's Guide to the 5 Love Languages®
by Gary Chapman with Paige Haley Drygas

The 5 Love Languages Singles® Edition
by Gary Chapman

The 5 Love Languages® Military Edition
by Gary Chapman & Jocelyn Green

God Speaks Your Love Language®
by Gary Chapman

Things I Wish I'd Known
Before We Became Parents
by Gary Chapman & Shannon Warden

Things I Wish I'd Known
Before My Child Became a Teenager
by Gary Chapman

Choose Greatness
by Gary Chapman & Clarence Shuler

SESSION 4

Initiating Positive Change

INSTRUCTIONS

Read through the Introduction below, either individually or aloud as a couple or group. Talk through the initial discussion questions together as you prepare to watch today's video. If you are going through this study on your own, consider journaling your responses in the pages included at the end of this Session Guide.

Introduction

Building a healthy family is an excellent goal, but it can be a lonely process.

Perhaps you're going through this study with your spouse. Maybe the two of you are just starting out in life, or maybe you're several years in and you've discovered that you need more support. Perhaps you're on this journey with a small group, but your spouse is gone or simply uninvolved. Or perhaps you're watching these videos by yourself, alone for the ride but eager to steer your family in a new direction.

If you and your spouse are on the same page when it comes to building a family, that's wonderful news. But many individuals start this process in a more divided state, looking woefully at past hurts and wishing desperately for something to change. Wherever you're coming from today, take heart. Even if it feels like you are the only one who cares about the health of your marriage and family, you can absolutely make a difference.

In today's session, we'll focus on how you can initiate positive change in your marriage—and consequently, in your whole family. We will explore some of Jesus' advice for relationship issues, drawing wisdom from Scripture and from Dr. Chapman's experience. Together, we will outline a practical plan of action, and as always, we will invite the Holy Spirit to be a central part of the process.

Before We Begin

Before we jump into today's video, take a few minutes to check in with your group or spouse (or consider your own thoughts). How would you describe the state of your marriage today? How would you like your marriage to look in the future? What are you most hoping to take away from today's session?

If you are going through this study as an individual, take a few minutes to consider and journal your responses.

Watch the Video

As you watch today's video, you may use the outline below to follow along or take notes. There are also journaling pages at the end of this Session Guide for further note-taking.

PLAY SESSION 4 VIDEO
"Initiating Positive Change"

SCRIPTURE FOR TODAY

Matthew 7:1–5 (NKJV)

"Judge not, that you be not judged. For with what judgment you judge, you will be judged; and with the measure you use, it will be measured back to you. And why do you look at the speck in your brother's eye, but do not consider the plank in your own eye? Or how can you say to your brother, 'Let me remove the speck from your eye'; and look, a plank is in your own eye? Hypocrite! First remove the plank from your own eye, and then you will see clearly to remove the speck from your brother's eye."

A **common response** is to describe the ________________________ in terms of my ____________________'s behavior.

Biblical Response

Practice

1. Prayer

"Lord, what is wrong with ___________?"

> *Let all bitterness, wrath, anger, clamor, and evil speaking be put away from you, with all malice. And be kind to one another, tenderhearted, forgiving one another, even as God in Christ forgave you.*
> **–Ephesians 4:31–32 (NKJV)**

2. Confession

Agree with God that:

- It is wrong
- Christ paid the penalty
- We will accept His forgiveness

> *If we confess our sins, He is faithful and just to forgive us our sins and to cleanse us from all unrighteousness.*
> **–1 John 1:9 (NKJV)**

3. Restitution

> *I myself always strive to have a conscience without offense toward God and men.*
> **–Acts 24:16 (NKJV)**

You are not responsible for **how your spouse responds.** The only sins you can ever deal with are your own.

How do I continue in growth?

A **common response** is: "Now, I will try harder!"

A **biblical response** is: be filled with the Holy Spirit

> *And do not be drunk with wine, in which is dissipation; but be filled with the Spirit.* **–Ephesians 5:18 (NKJV)**

Ministry of the Holy Spirit

1. The Holy Spirit ______________________ all Christians.

> *But you are not in the flesh but in the Spirit, if indeed the Spirit of God dwells in you. Now if anyone does not have the Spirit of Christ, he is not His.*
> **–Romans 8:9 (NKJV)**

2. The Holy Spirit ______________________ us when we do wrong.

> *And you have forgotten the exhortation which speaks to you as to sons: "My son, do not despise the chastening of the LORD, nor be discouraged when you are rebuked by Him."* **–Hebrews 12:5 (NKJV)**

3. The Holy Spirit ______________________ us of the truth.

> *However, when He, the Spirit of truth, has come, He will guide you into all truth; for He will not speak on His own authority, but whatever He hears He will speak; and He will tell you things to come.*
> **–John 16:13 (NKJV)**

4. The Holy Spirit ______________________ us.

> *And I will pray the Father, and He will give you another Helper, that He may abide with you forever.*
> **–John 14:16 (NKJV)**

5. The Holy Spirit ________________________ the qualities of Christ through us.

> *But the fruit of the Spirit is love, joy, peace, longsuffering, kindness, goodness, faithfulness, gentleness, self-control. Against such there is no law.*
> **–Galatians 5:22–23 (NKJV)**

Two Essentials

1. ______________________ the Holy Spirit.
2. ______________________ to His control.

Let's Talk About It

QUESTION #1: In today's video, Dr. Chapman acknowledged our human tendency to blame most of the problems in marriage on our spouses. Even with this being the case, how can we begin to address our marriage issues? Why do you think Dr. Chapman referenced Matthew 7:1–5 in introducing this idea?

QUESTION #2: As a group, review aloud Dr. Chapman's practical process for initiating positive change in marriage. What resonates with you about this process? What might be challenging about putting it into practice?
TIP: *See the video outline in the previous pages to refresh your memory.*

QUESTION #3: Think back to Dr. Chapman's story from the end of today's video, when he shared about what really saved his marriage. What do you think it looks like to have the attitude of Christ? What might this look like in your marriage (or in marriage in general)?

QUESTION #4: What were the three practical questions Dr. Chapman began to ask his wife in his pursuit of developing an attitude of Christ toward her? If you were to start asking your spouse these questions, what do you imagine might happen?

QUESTION #5: Take a few minutes of your group time for silent introspection as you consider what it means to be filled and directed by the Holy Spirit in everyday life (Ephesians 5:18). Consider, perhaps, the state of your spiritual life in general. What is your spiritual life like these days, and how does it affect other areas of your daily life?
TIP: *This is a deep and significant topic, but it's one worth addressing in your pursuit of a healthy family. For now, consider*

journaling your initial thoughts in the empty pages at the end of this Session Guide. Groups are encouraged to return to this topic during the prayer time as well.

To Wrap It Up

In today's discussion time, we asked the questions: *What does it mean to be filled and directed by the Holy Spirit? What is the state of my spiritual life in general?* These are deeply personal questions, perhaps ones you aren't comfortable answering aloud today. But as Dr. Chapman shared, it's no coincidence that when he was willing to adopt the attitude of Christ toward his wife, his marriage began to change for the better. If we want to effect positive change in our marriages, we must first take an honest look at ourselves, truthfully considering our willingness to invite God into the mess.

Maybe you don't feel that you have a spiritual life at all—or you may even feel hurt or distaste for the idea. What brought on these feelings in your life? Maybe you've gone to church for as long as you can remember, but your faith doesn't seem to go far beyond that. If you are honest with yourself, do you see your choices and behaviors being consistently directed by the Holy Spirit? Or is there some level of separation between your church and home lives?

Maybe, like Dr. Chapman, you have witnessed firsthand the good that comes out of truly giving your heart to Christ, allowing His attitude to permeate each area of your life. As we discovered in today's video, initiating positive change in marriage begins with addressing our own failures—and this is not something that we can accomplish without God's help. As you continue in your journey toward building a healthy family, take as much time as you need to evaluate your own heart.

Pray About It

Consider concluding this session in prayer. This can look like any number of things—praying or prayer journaling individually; praying aloud as a couple; or praying for one another's requests as a group. But remember, the One who created families in the first place is the One who is best equipped to help you!

Feel free to use the following prompts, should you find them helpful:

- Recalling our initial discussions from before watching today's video, spend time praying for each other's marriages, inviting the Holy Spirit into the process. Remember, this can be a painful topic for many people, so we should be kindly aware of each person's needs.
- Take time to talk and pray with one another about each person's relationship with God. Remember to give space and grace to each person in your group, as each is coming to this study from different places in the journey.
- If there are any other family concerns among you, take time to discuss and pray over one other. Consider how you might support one another in practical ways as you continue in this study.

More from Dr. Chapman

Below are the three questions that Dr. Chapman recommends asking your spouse regularly in order to begin adopting the attitude of Christ in your marriage. Consider printing these out or keeping them written down in a handy place, where you can remind yourself to put this into practice.

1. What can I do to help you?
2. How can I make your life easier?
3. How can I be a better spouse?

Notes & Journaling

Feel free to use this space to take notes or journal your thoughts from today's session.

Book Recommendations

If you would like to dig deeper into how to build healthy family relationships, consider some new reading material! Each of these titles can be found at **5LoveLanguages.com.**

Seen. Known. Loved.
5 Truths About God and Your Love Language®
by Gary Chapman & R. York Moore

5 Simple Ways to Strengthen Your Marriage
. . . When You're Stuck at Home Together
by Gary Chapman

Married and Still Loving It:
The Joys and Challenge of the Second Half
by Gary Chapman & Harold Myra

One More Try:
What to Do When Your Marriage Is Falling Apart
by Gary Chapman

Loving Your Spouse When You Feel Like Walking Away:
Real Help for Desperate Hearts in Difficult Marriages
by Gary Chapman

Holding on to Love After You've Lost a Baby
by Gary Chapman & Candy McVicar

The Love Language® Devotional Bible
by Gary Chapman

Your New Life with Adult Children:
A Practical Guide to What Helps, What Hurts, and What Heals
by Gary Chapman & Ross Campbell

SESSION 5

Anger: How to Tame a Powerful Emotion

INSTRUCTIONS

Read through the Introduction below, either individually or aloud as a couple or group. Talk through the initial discussion questions together as you prepare to watch today's video. If you are going through this study on your own, consider journaling your responses in the pages included at the end of this Session Guide.

Introduction

They say love is the most powerful emotion—and that's true! The Bible says that it was for love of us that Jesus died on the cross to redeem humanity. "Love never fails," the apostle Paul wrote to the Corinthian believers (1 Corinthians 13:8 NIV).

But in our lived human experience, if love is the most *powerful* emotion, anger might just seem like the most *frequently occurring* one.

How many times do you find yourself growing angry over various things throughout the day? What typically sets you off? How do you express your anger? As a Christian, you may even be worried about how often you feel the emotion of anger. *Isn't anger a bad thing? How am I* still *dealing with these feelings if I have the Holy Spirit helping me?*

Many of us have grown accustomed to masking our anger in more public spaces, such as at work or with people outside the family. After all, it's not professional to "lose it," right? But it's less easy to control those feelings at home with the family. In a marriage, it can seem downright impossible.

So, how in the world are we supposed to tame this emotion?

In today's session, we will look at the source of anger, understanding its origins and intended purpose. We will define the different types of anger that we experience, discussing what triggers our anger and how to approach it. Finally, we will draw from Dr. Chapman's years of counseling experience to outline a practical plan for the next time we get angry, equipping ourselves with the tools we need to process anger in a healthy way.

Before We Begin

Before we jump into today's video, take a few minutes to check in with your group or spouse (or consider your own thoughts). How do you tend to react when you are angry? How does your spouse usually react? How have you seen these habits affect your family relationships?

If you are going through this study as an individual, take a few minutes to consider and journal your responses.

Watch the Video

As you watch today's video, you may use the outline below to follow along or take notes. There are also journaling pages at the end of this Session Guide for further note-taking.

PLAY SESSION 5 VIDEO

"Anger: How to Tame a Powerful Emotion"

The Source of Anger

Anger is rooted in the nature of God.

God is love, but God experiences anger.

> *But anyone who does not love does not know God, for God is love.* **– 1 John 4:8 (NLT)**

God wants us to have the best possible lives, and He experiences anger when He sees us hurting ourselves and others.

Why do we experience anger?

We are made in the ____________________ of God.

> *So God created human beings in his own image. In the image of God he created them; male and female he created them.* **– Genesis 1:27 (NLT)**

Therefore, we have a concern for right and wrong.

The Purpose of Anger

To ____________________ us to take constructive ____________________.

Two Types of Human Anger

______________________________ anger: a wrong has been committed

But when Peter came to Antioch, I had to oppose him to his face, for what he did was very wrong. When he first arrived, he ate with the Gentile believers, who were not circumcised. But afterward, when some friends of James came, Peter wouldn't eat with the Gentiles anymore. He was afraid of criticism from these people who insisted on the necessity of circumcision. As a result, other Jewish believers followed Peter's hypocrisy, and even Barnabas was led astray by their hypocrisy. When I saw that they were not following the truth of the gospel message, I said to Peter in front of all the others, "Since you, a Jew by birth, have discarded the Jewish laws and are living like a Gentile, why are you now trying to make these Gentiles follow the Jewish traditions?"
–Galatians 2:11–14 (NLT)

_________________________ anger: no wrong has been committed

Abel also brought a gift—the best portions of the firstborn lambs from his flock. The LORD accepted Abel and his gift, but he did not accept Cain and his gift. This made Cain very angry, and he looked dejected. "Why are you so angry?" the LORD asked Cain. "Why do you look so dejected? You will be accepted if you do what is right. But if you refuse to do what is right, then watch out! Sin is crouching at the door, eager to control you. But you must subdue it and be its master."
–Genesis 4:4–7 (NLT)

How to Process Anger

1. ______________________________ your anger.

> *And "don't sin by letting anger control you." Don't let the sun go down while you are still angry . . .*
> **–Ephesians 4:26 (NLT)**

2. ______________________________ your immediate response.

> *Sensible people control their temper; they earn respect by overlooking wrongs* **–Proverbs 19:11 (NLT)**

3. Locate the ______________________________ of your anger.

Why am I angry? What kind of anger am I experiencing?

If it is **distorted** anger: confess it as ________________________.

> *Always be humble and gentle. Be patient with each other, making allowance for each other's faults because of your love.* **–Ephesians 4:2 (NLT)**

If it is **definitive** anger: take ______________________________ action.

- Lovingly ____________________________ the offender.

So watch yourselves! If another believer sins, rebuke that person; then if there is repentance, forgive. Even if that person wrongs you seven times a day and each time turns again and asks forgiveness, you must forgive. **–Luke 17:3–4 (NLT)**

Dear brothers and sisters, if another believer is overcome by some sin, you who are godly should gently and humbly help that person back onto the right path. And be careful not to fall into the same temptation yourself. **–Galatians 6:1 (NLT)**

- ______________________ the person and your anger to God.
- Return ______________________ for evil.

Dear friends, never take revenge. Leave that to the righteous anger of God. For the Scriptures say, "I will take revenge; I will pay them back," says the LORD. Instead, "If your enemies are hungry, feed them. If they are thirsty, give them something to drink. In doing this, you will heap burning coals of shame on their heads." Don't let evil conquer you, but conquer evil by doing good. **–Romans 12:19–21 (NLT)**

Challenge

Learn to use the ______________________ of anger to further the cause of ______________________ in the world.

Let's Talk About It

QUESTION #1: Where does anger come from? Why does God experience anger? Why do we as human beings experience anger?

QUESTION #2: What is the difference between definitive and distorted anger? What examples of each can you think of from your own life?

QUESTION #3: What most often triggers feelings of anger (either definitive or distorted) in your family relationships, and why? How have you handled these situations in the past? What does expressing anger usually look like in your marriage or family at present?

QUESTION #4: As a group, review together the steps to process anger in a healthy way. Which step seems to come most naturally to you? Which do you find most challenging, and why?

QUESTION #5: Going forward, how do you hope to use today's session to guide conflict resolution in your marriage and family? How would you like others to pray for you on this topic?

TO WRAP IT UP

Many of us grew up suffering the consequences of mismanaged anger, whether from parents, other relatives, or even teachers and coaches. As an adult, perhaps your most natural inclination is to explode when the feeling hits you, or perhaps you shrink and bottle the feelings up tight. Maybe you *did* have healthy role models when it came to expressing anger, but now it's your turn to figure out how to navigate this in your own family. For many of us, anger can feel like the most challenging emotion to deal with when it comes to building a healthy family. But remember, you're not alone in feeling this way!

No matter what experiences we bring to the table, we do not have to live in fear of letting our anger get the best of us. We do not have to carry guilt for feeling anger in the first place, and we *can* learn to express it in a healthy way. Anger is a powerful emotion, but it doesn't have to be an uncontrollable one.

As we prepare to conclude our session, take time to pray for one another's needs in this area. If you are going through this study with your spouse, make a practical plan for how to deal with feelings of anger the next time you find yourselves in conflict. If not, consider forming your own plan based on today's session, and discuss it with your spouse or family when the time seems right.

Pray About It

Consider concluding this session in prayer. This can look like any number of things—praying or prayer journaling individually; praying aloud as a couple; or praying for one another's requests as a group. But remember, the One who created families in the first place is the One who is best equipped to help you!

Feel free to use the following prompts, should you find them helpful:

- Consider which step from Dr. Chapman's process of handling anger you find most challenging. Take time to pray for one another regarding these steps, asking the Holy Spirit to help each person begin to manage anger in a healthy way.

- If there are any specific issues regarding anger in the family, spend time in prayer for one another. Consider practical ways to support each other in this area.
- If there are any other family concerns among you, take time to discuss and pray over one other. Consider how you might practically support one another as you continue in this study.

More from Dr. Chapman

To dig deeper into the topic of managing anger, check out Dr. Chapman's book *Anger: Taming a Powerful Emotion*, which is available at **5LoveLanguages.com.**

How to Process Our Anger
As you practice processing your anger in a healthy way, here is a quick cheat sheet of the steps that Dr. Chapman outlined in today's video:

STEP #1: **Admit you are angry.**

STEP #2: **Restrain your immediate response.** If needed, call "Time Out" and remove yourself from the situation so you can clear your head.

STEP #3: **Locate the source of your anger.** Why am I angry? Is this definitive anger, where a wrong was committed, or is it distorted anger, where no wrong was committed?

STEP #4: **If it's distorted anger, confess it to God.** Ask for His help as you plan how to respond.

STEP #5: **If it's definitive anger, lovingly confront the offender.** You may need to take a few more minutes to cool off and pray about what to say before you take this step.

STEP #6: If the person who has wronged you does not repent, **release them to God and return good for evil.**

Notes & Journaling

Feel free to use this space to take notes or journal your thoughts from today's session.

Book Recommendations

If you would like to dig deeper into how to build healthy family relationships, consider some new reading material! Each of these titles can be found at **5LoveLanguages.com.**

Anger: Taming a Powerful Emotion
by Gary Chapman

The 5 Apology Languages
by Gary Chapman & Jennifer Thomas

One More Try:
What to Do When Your Marriage Is Falling Apart
by Gary Chapman

Loving Your Spouse When You Feel Like Walking Away:
Real Help for Desperate Hearts in Difficult Marriages
by Gary Chapman

SESSION 6

The 5 Apology Languages

INSTRUCTIONS

Read through the Introduction below, either individually or aloud as a couple or group. Talk through the initial discussion questions together as you prepare to watch today's video. If you are going through this study on your own, consider journaling your responses in the pages included at the end of this Session Guide.

Introduction

We introduced Session 1 of this study by acknowledging a harsh reality: There is no such thing as a perfect family. Now that we've made it to our final session, it's time for yet another round of bad news:

You are going to fail.

Now, don't toss this study guide across the room just yet—you haven't made it all the way to Session 6 for nothing. The point is: None of us are perfect. No matter how hard we try, we are simply going to make mistakes along the way. If we want to build healthy families, not only do we need to make sure each member feels loved; we also need to know how to deal with our mistakes when we (inevitably) make them.

Just as having an attitude of service informs each of the other characteristics of a healthy family, **knowing how to acknowledge and deal with our failures** informs our ability to express love in meaningful ways.

In our final session, Dr. Chapman will introduce the idea of the 5 Apology Languages, unpacking how we can learn to make things right with our loved ones in ways that they find most sincere. We will talk about the role of mercy in resolving conflicts, recognizing what forgiveness *does* and *does not do* when it comes to relationships. And finally, we will process what we *are* and *are not* responsible for when it comes to dealing with our own failures—and those of our loved ones.

Before We Begin

Before we jump into today's video, take a few minutes to check in with your group or spouse (or consider your own thoughts). When you apologize, what do you typically say or do? When someone is apologizing to you, what do you want to hear *them* say or do? Discuss as a group, noting each person's different preferences.

If you are going through this study as an individual, take a few minutes to consider and journal your responses.

Watch the Video

As you watch today's video, you may use the outline below to follow along or take notes. There are also journaling pages at the end of this Session Guide for further note-taking.

PLAY SESSION 6 VIDEO

"The 5 Apology Languages"

Two Essentials for Successful Relationships

1. That the individuals feel ________________ and appreciated.
2. That the individuals deal effectively with their ________________________.

The 5 Apology Languages

1. **Expressing** ______________________

Use the words, **"I'm sorry . . ."**

—but don't stop there! Tell them what you are sorry for.

Never say, **"I'm sorry, *but* . . ."**

This is not an apology! Adding a "but" places the blame for your poor behavior on your loved one.

2. **Accepting** ______________________

This language includes admitting, "I was wrong."

3. **Making** ______________________

For some people, the question, "What can I do to make this right?" indicates a sincere apology.

4. **Genuinely** ______________________

The word repent means "to turn away from."

This language includes both **expressing a desire to change** AND **actually changing the behavior.**

5. **Requesting** ______________________

For some people, specifically requesting their forgiveness is necessary for a sincere apology.

Each of us has a **primary apology language.**

If you want to communicate your ______________________, you must speak the other person's language.

Discovering Your Primary Apology Language

To identify your primary apology language, start by asking yourself a few questions:

1. When I apologize, what do I typically say or do?
2. What hurts me most deeply about this situation?
3. What could they say or do that would make it easier for me to forgive?

Learning to Forgive

The **biblical response** to an apology is ______________________.

Forgiveness offers mercy instead of justice, removes the emotional barrier that prevents us from moving on.

What forgiveness ***does not*** do:

1. Forgiveness does not ______________________ our memory.
2. Forgiveness does not remove all painful ________________.
3. Forgiveness does not remove all the ________________ of sin.
4. Forgiveness does not ___________________________ trust.
5. Forgiveness does not always result in ________________.

What if the person does not apologize?

1. We lovingly ______________________.

> *"If another believer sins against you, go privately and point out the offense. If the other person listens and confesses it, you have won that person back. But if you are unsuccessful, take one or two others with you and go back again, so that everything you say may be confirmed by two or three witnesses. If the person still refuses to listen, take your case to the church. Then if he or she won't accept the church's decision, treat that person as a pagan or a corrupt tax collector."*
> **– Matthew 18:15–17 (NLT)**

1. We ______________________ the person to God.
2. We ______________________ for them and stand ready to ______________________.
3. We return ______________________ for evil.

> *Do not take revenge, my dear friends, but leave room for God's wrath, for it is written: "It is mine to avenge; I will repay," says the Lord. On the contrary: "If your enemy is hungry, feed him; if he is thirsty, give him something to drink. In doing this, you will heap burning coals on his head." Do not be overcome by evil, but overcome evil with good.* **– Romans 12:19–21 (NIV)**

Let's Talk About It

QUESTION #1: Let's recap—what are the 5 Apology Languages? What might a sincere apology look like in each of these languages?

QUESTION #2: What resonated most with you from today's video? What do you find most difficult or challenging about dealing with your failures in your own family relationships?

QUESTION #3: Thinking back to our discussion before the video, what do you suspect might be your primary Apology Language (or your top two)? Why is this method of apology most meaningful to you? Discuss as a group.
TIP: As you consider this question, refer back to the video outline in the previous pages for help in determining possible primary languages.

QUESTION #4: As we conclude our time together, think back to each session of this group study. Which sessions or ideas resonated most with you? Discuss as a group.

QUESTION #5: Continuing to recall each of the six sessions of this study, which areas are you most eager to begin improving upon in your family? What do you find most challenging, and what would you like prayer for?

To Wrap It Up

Much of our time in this study has been spent learning how to sincerely express love—but in a healthy family, it's just as important to sincerely address our failures! When we are able to acknowledge our mistakes and meaningfully address them in our relationships, we are that much more equipped to build the kind of family that lasts.

Congratulations, friend—you have successfully journeyed through all six sessions of our time together. Throughout this group study, we have:

- Unpacked **five traits of a healthy family**;
- Discovered the **5 Love Languages® of our children**, and explored how to speak them;
- Created a personal plan for **initiating positive change** in marriage—even if we have to do it alone;
- Learned how to **process different types of anger** in healthy ways; and
- Explored how to use the **5 Apology Languages** in dealing with our failures, which is essential for all forms of healthy relationships.

With each of these skills in your tool belt, you have everything you need to start growing the kind of family you've always wanted. May God bless you with His wisdom and discernment as you start to build—not a *perfect* family—but one that is perfectly equipped to face whatever life throws at you *together*.

Now, get out there and start building!

Pray About It

Consider concluding this session in prayer. This can look like any number of things—praying or prayer journaling individually; praying aloud as a couple; or praying for one another's requests as a group. But remember, the One who created families in the first place is the One who is best equipped to help you!

Feel free to use the following prompts, should you find them helpful:

- Spend time praying in general for each family represented in your group (or over your own family).
- Recalling the answers to today's discussion questions, spend time in prayer for each person's specific needs.
- If there are any other family concerns among you, take time to discuss and pray over one other. Consider how you might continue to support one another in practical ways, even as our study time comes to an end.

More from Dr. Chapman

Read the Book

If you would like to dig deeper into the 5 Apology Languages, check out the book! *The 5 Apology Languages* by Gary Chapman and Jennifer Thomas is available at **5LoveLanguages.com**.

Take the Quiz

Still not sure what your primary Apology Language might be? You can take the free Apology Languages quiz on the 5 Love Languages® website: https://5lovelanguages.com/quizzes/apology-language

Make It Personal

Dealing with our failures can be intimidating, but it's always worth it. If today's session really hit home, consider taking some time in private to process the following questions. Feel free to make use of the journal pages at the end of this Session Guide.

1. Whom do I need to forgive today?
2. Whom do I need to lovingly confront?
3. Whom do I need to release to God?
4. To whom do I need to apologize?

Notes & Journaling

Feel free to use this space to take notes or journal your thoughts from today's session.

Book Recommendations

If you would like to dig deeper into how to build healthy family relationships, consider some new reading material! Each of these titles can be found at **5LoveLanguages.com**.

Anger: Taming a Powerful Emotion
by Gary Chapman

The 5 Apology Languages
by Gary Chapman & Jennifer Thomas

One More Try:
What to Do When Your Marriage Is Falling Apart
by Gary Chapman

Loving Your Spouse When You Feel Like Walking Away:
Real Help for Desperate Hearts in Difficult Marriages
by Gary Chapman